WISCONSIN

"JOGRAPHY"

A Fun Run Through Our State!
by
Carole Marsh

This activity book has material which correlates with Wisconsin's Model Academic Standards for Social Studies. At every opportunity, we have tried to relate information to the History and Social Science, English, Science, Math, Civics, Economics, and Computer Technology Model directives. For additional information, go to our websites: **www.thewisconsinexperience.com** or **www.gallopade.com**.

Gallopade is proud to be a member of these educational organizations and associations:

The Wisconsin Experience Series

The Wisconsin Experience! Paperback Book

My First Pocket Guide to Wisconsin!

The Big Wisconsin Reproducible Activity Book

The Wisconsin Coloring Book!

My First Book About Wisconsin!

Wisconsin Jeopardy: Answers & Questions About Our State

Wisconsin "Jography!": A Fun Run Through Our State

The Wisconsin Experience! Sticker Pack

The Wisconsin Experience! Poster/Map

Discover Wisconsin CD-ROM

Wisconsin "GEO" Bingo Game

Wisconsin "HISTO" Bingo Game

Table of Contents

What is "Jography"?

Dear Parent, Teacher, Librarian, and other readers,

Haven't you ever heard a kid pronounce geography jooography—as in, "I have lots of "jography" homework but I left my jooography book at school and we have a jooography test tomorrow!"

From the reports that we read, that kid may very well flunk that "jography" test. What a shame that such a vital, interesting, essential subject has been so short-changed. Why is this? Perhaps we thought geography was boring when we were in school. Maybe it seems to change too much. Just when we figure out where a country is, it changes its name, capital, and government! Or are we not willing or able to visualize the world as what it is—just a big neighborhood?

Whatever the reason, I hope my series of "Jography" books help make geography more exciting and interesting. Never before has geography been a more important study for students. Through political and environmental concerns, we have found just how important it is for us to know where our neighbors are and what they are up to. And the world is growing economically smaller. A child's future career may take them further than around the block! They are almost bound to be involved with other countries and their language, cultures, and money.

But the best place to start is out our own back door! Perhaps geography does seem boring or useless until someone gives us season passes to our favorite team's games. Then all we have to do is figure out how to get there. Now that's motivation!

So, the approach this book takes is to consider geography from the kid's point of view—what they may be interested in, plus to communicate that geography is history, economics, politics, art, science, communication, etc.

Thank you for helping kids get hooked on "jography"!

Carole Marsh

WHERE AM I?

Some Down-to-Earth Reasons to Know Your "Jography"

Recent studies show most people know very little about the places in the world in which they live.

Sometimes it's as important to know where somewhere isn't, as much as where it is (unless you like catching the right plane to the wrong destination or vice versa!).

If you don't want to learn too much about a place, at least hit the high spots so you won't sound dumb or insult someone. But even more importantly, go ahead and learn a lot about a place you're interested in. After all, in today's truly global economy, there's just no telling where in the world you'll find yourself calling on the phone, putting money in the bank, or traveling to by plane, boat, or rickshaw!

What's "Jography"? It's a way to explore a place that's just a little more realistic and a little more fun. Most people don't even know much about the geography of their state until someone gives them free tickets to the big game—now all they have to do is figure out how to get there! And I'll bet if they announced there was money growing on trees in Kalamazoo, you'd have no trouble finding out exactly where it is!

So, put on your jogging shoes, lace 'em up tight and let's go on an armchair journey. Like any true traveler and serious geographer—of course you can use a map! Look in an encyclopedia, atlas, or ask your parent or teacher until you find a map that you like and that makes sense to you. Then see if you find the answers to some of the following questions. I'll bet you discover them and a whole lot more!

Happy "Jographing"! And for fun—keep score!

Wisconsin "Jography" Word Search

Before you get started, jog your memory! You've heard of most of the geography-related words below. Find them in this word search. Hint: You'll only find them by latitude and longitude! Score one point for each word discovered.

```
C H A R T X L I D E G R E E O C E A N
O P O L E Z R H E Q U A T O R X B M N
N D G L A C I E R X U I S L A N D N B
T E M O U N T A I N R U Y L A K E M O
I S A R C T I C P L C I V O L M R J A
N E R I V E R X J O V W I N D U R P C
E R T D E L T A Z N E G L O B E M R S
N T I Z O N E L M G R V O L C A N O X
T R O P I C S X C I B E A R T H M A P
G L V J S B V M K T I D E W A T E R L
V V A P S L P P L U C L W Q P M F C A
D U B L A T I T U D E P I E D M O N T
P T N A L L X I N E W Z M R P O I U E
O G R I D E V K J H R E G I O N S P A
X P E N I N S U L A M N B C X H G E U
```

Word Bank

CHART   DEGREE   OCEAN   POLE   LATITUDE   EQUATOR   GLACIER   ISLAND

MOUNTAIN   LAKE   ARCTIC   WIND   DELTA   GLOBE   ZONE   VOLCANO

TROPICS   EARTH   CONTINENT   DESERT   RIVER   LONGITUDE   TIDEWATER

PIEDMONT   PLAIN   PENINSULA   GRID   PLATEAU   REGIONS   MAP

Wisconsin
"Jography" Comes in All Flavors!

Match the type of geography with the area of study it would cover. Score one point for each correct answer. Be sure to cover the bottom of the sheet until you have your answers!

Branch

1. Geography
2. Physiography
3. Mathematical geography
4. Biogeography
5. Oceanography
6. Meteorology
7. Economic geography
8. Anthropography
9. Climatology
10. Political geography

Study

A. Land forms
B. Weather forecasting
C. The physical Earth
D. People and geography
E. Plants, animals
F. Parallels, meridians
G. Waves, tides, currents
H. Industry location
I. Government boundaries
J. Weather

I WANT TO BE A WEATHERMAN!

MY SCORE _____

ANSWERS: 1-C; 2-A; 3-F; 4-E; 5-G; 6-B; 7-H; 8-D; 9-J; 10-I

Wisconsin
Our State from A-To-Z!

This should give you a good overview of your state. Take your map and see if you can find a mountain, river, or place for each letter of the alphabet listed here. Score one point for each. (Score two points if you find a Q, U, X, Y, Z!)

A_____
B_____
C_____
D_____
E_____
F_____
G_____
H_____
I_____
J_____
K_____
L_____
M_____
N_____
O_____
P_____
QUICK, YOU'RE DOING GREAT!_____
R_____
S_____
T_____
U CAN DO IT!_____
V_____
W_____
X_____
Y_____
Z_____

MY_____ SCORE

Hitting the High Spots!

For a quick overview of the cities and towns you might pass through on a fast trip through Wisconsin—hop in your car and take the trip below. Score a point for each city you can name. Hey—and watch that speed limit!!

North to South and East to West

1. Milwaukee

    A. The city halfway up Lake Winnebago known for its rugged clothing

2. Oshkosh

    B. The third largest and oldest city in the state

3. Appleton

    C. A snowmobiler's paradise

4. La Crosse

    D. The largest city, a Great Lake port, and industrial center

5. Baraboo

    E. People come to catch "the big one" here, just off Lake Michigan

6. Green Bay

    F. Named for the Native American game lacrosse

7. New Glarus

    G. "Paper Valley" where several paper mills are located

8. Madison

    H. The state capital and a main cultural center

9. Kenosha

    I. Home to the Circus World Museum

10. Eagle River

    J. Little Switzerland is here with its Swiss influence

ANSWERS: 1-D; 2-A; 3-G; 4-F; 5-I; 6-B; 7-J; 8-H; 9-E; 10-C

IS IT OVER YET?

MY SCORE _____

Wisconsin
The Great Escape!

Hop on your bike and take a tour of these Wisconsin landmarks and attractions. Score a point for each one you match correctly.

What A Workout!

1. Lake Geneva

2. Hayward

3. Door County

4. Bristol

5. Elkhart Lake

6. Mineral Point

7. Near Dodgeville

8. Racine

9. West Bend

10. Prairie du Chien

A. A very popular tourist destination

B. A thirteen-sided barn can be viewed here, built in 1915

C. Home to many large, beautiful, and luxurious older homes

D. Cornish and Irish miners worked the lead mines

E. Home to the household appliance manufacturer

F. Home of the National Freshwater Fishing Hall of Fame

G. A major Renaissance Fair is held here every summer

H. Famous for its yummy Danish kringles

I. Villa Louis, mansion of the first millionaire in Wisconsin

J. House on the Rock

I ESCAPED!

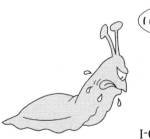

MY SCORE

ANSWERS: 1-C; 2-F; 3-A; 4-G; 5-B; 6-D; 7-J; 8-H; 9-E; 10-I

Over the River and Through the Woods

See if you can figure out which Wisconsin river, lake, or forest we're trying to locate. Score one point for each right answer!

Keep An Eye To The Sky!

1. Horicon Marsh

A. Where the glacier missed in the Baraboo Hills leaving a lake

2. Peshtigo River

B. The state's longest river

3. The North Woods

C. Fifty miles square (129 sq km), result of a retreating glacier

4. Lake Winnebago

D. River with rippling, rushing falls

5. Hills of Trempealeau

E. The northern region of the state full of pines, lakes, and streams

6. Amnicon River

F. Largest lake within Wisconsin, known to be shallow

7. Wisconsin River

G. Range of stone peaks carved by the Mississippi River

8. Lake Superior

H. A rafter's rippling ride down this river is fun in the spring!

9. Chequamegon National Forest

I. Stretches from the far north of the state south to Medford, an off-road bicycler's dream!

10. Devil's Lake

J. Largest freshwater lake in the world which lies to the north

MY _____
SCORE

ANSWERS: 1-C; 2-H; 3-E; 4-F; 5-G; 6-D; 7-B; 8-J; 9-I; 10-A

Wisconsin
State Borders

Wisconsin is surrounded by several other states. Can you name Wisconsin's borders? Score one point for each border you match.

1. Illinois

2. Minnesota

3. Michigan

4. Lake Michigan

5. Iowa

6. Lake Superior

A. A Great Lake with a bordering state's name, to the east

B. This neighbor is to the northeast, home of Detroit

C. The "best" lake to the north

D. Chicago is this neighbor's largest city

E. A neighbor to the west known for its many lakes

F. Amana Colonies are in this neighboring state

HEEEY! WAIT FOR ME!

SEE YOU AROUND!

MY SCORE _____

ANSWERS: 1-D; 2-E; 3-B; 4-A; 5-F; 6-C

A Few of My Favorite People, Places, and Things

I'll bet they are yours too! But who, what, and where are they?
Score a point for each one you match correctly.

Fun! Fun! Fun! Fun!

1. Milwaukee

2. Cedar Creek Settlement

3. Aztalan

4. Carrie Chapman Catt

5. Honeybee

6. Shirley S. Abrahamson

7. Zona Gale

8. Green Bay Packers

9. Ezekiel Gillespie

10. Al Capone

A. German stone barns and half-timber houses built in the mid-1800s are found here

B. Helped blacks win the right to vote in the state

C. Nicknamed "Cream City" for its production of yellow-colored bricks

D. A writer who supported women's rights and equality issues

E. The state's insect that loves clover

F. Fought for women's right to vote

G. Organized in 1919 by "Curly" Lambeau

H. Mysterious remains of an ancient Indian village, northernmost in North America

I. First woman to serve on the state's supreme court

J. Maintained a hideaway at Couderay, near Hayward

ANSWERS: 1-C; 2-A; 3-H; 4-F; 5-E; 6-I; 7-D; 8-G; 9-B; 10-J

Wisconsin
School Daze!

If someone gave you season tickets to a game or activity of the schools below—would you know where to find them? Score a point for each match.

Rah! Rah!! Rah!!!

1. University of Wisconsin Outreach School of Arts

2. Nashotah House

3. University of Wisconsin

4. Watertown

5. Lawrence University

6. Carroll College

7. Kenosha

8. "The University"

A. As an Indian mission and seminary, it's the oldest institution of higher learning

B. The oldest private college in the state

C. The first free elementary school was founded here in 1845

D. Coeducational school in Appleton since 1847

E. The first kindergarten in the U.S. was established here

F. A popular writing and art learning center in Rhinelander

G. University of Wisconsin at Madison

H. A huge top-rated public university system in the state

MY SCORE _____

ANSWERS: 1-F; 2-A; 3-H; 4-E; 5-D; 6-B; 7-C; 8-G

Wisconsin

Road Rally!

This is like a scavenger hunt by car! Here are the places on your list. Score a point for each name you complete. Good luck!

RRRROAD RRRRALLY!

1. It's not a car or truck but a mini: Dela _ _ _

2. Furniture with drawers for your clothes: _ _ _ _ _ _ er

3. On a cliff, don't stand too close to the: _ _ _ _ rton

4. Where the dust always collects: Hales _ _ _ _ _ _ _

5. You put your shoe or sandal over this: _ _ _ _ ville

6. A gentleman opens the door for a: _ _ _ _ smith

7. No frills, simple at its best: _ _ _ _ _ field

8. What you eat ice cream with: _ _ _ _ _ er

9. A beautiful flower, grows on a bush: Wild _ _ _ _

10. This city "bends" away from the east: _ _ _ _ Bend

MY SCORE

ANSWERS: 1-Delavan; 2-Dresser; 3-Edgerton; 4-Hales Corners; 5-Footville; 6-Ladysmith; 7-Plainfield; 8-Spooner; 9-Wild Rose; 10-West Bend

Wisconsin
Stand Up and Be County-ed!

Score a point for each city you can correctly match with its county.

I'm County-ing On You

1. Sauk
2. Oneida
3. Walworth
4. Grant
5. Bayfield
6. Langlade
7. Grecn
8. Racine
9. Jefferson
10. Wood

A. Rhinelander
B. Monroe
C. Elkhorn
D. Baraboo
E. Platteville
F. Watertown
G. Burlington
H. Antigo
I. Marshfield
J. Ashland

GATORADE!
GATORADE!

MY _____ SCORE

ANSWERS: 1-D; 2-A; 3-C; 4-E; 5-J; 6-H; 7-B; 8-G; 9-F; 10-I

Wisconsin
Two-Name Places

How many of these two-name places can you figure out? Score one point for each one you can match correctly.

Two For The Price Of One!

1. Beaver
2. Lake
3. Green
4. Eau
5. New

A. Dam
B. London
C. Claire
D. Bay
E. Geneva

Help Beaver find his way through the maze to connect with Dam to become the city of _ _ _ _ _ _ _   _ _ _!

MY SCORE ____

Wisconsin
Instant "Fax!"

There are always a few simple facts about our state we are sure we know. See if that's true! Score one point for each correct fact!

FACTS 'R US!

OFFICIAL NAME: _____

IS THE: _____TH STATE/YEAR: _____

CAPITAL: _____FOUNDED: _____

STATE NICKNAME: _____

STATE MOTTO: _____

STATE BIRD: _____

STATE DOG: _____

STATE FISH: _____

STATE ANIMAL: _____

STATE DOMESTICATED ANIMAL: _____

STATE WILDLIFE ANIMAL: _____

STATE INSECT: _____

STATE TREE: _____

STATE FLOWER: _____

STATE ROCK: _____

STATE FOSSIL: _____

STATE SONG: _____

STATE MINERAL: _____

STATE GRAIN: _____

STATE BEVERAGE: _____

HIGHEST POINT: _____

NUMBER OF COUNTIES: _____

ANSWERS: Wisconsin; 30th; 1848; Madison; 1836; Badger State and America's Dairyland; "Forward"; Robin; American water spaniel; Muskellunge; Badger; Dairy cow; White-tailed deer; Honeybee; Sugar maple; Wood violet; Red granite; Trilobite; "On, Wisconsin!"; Galena; Corn; Milk; Timms Hill, 1,952 feet (595 m); 72

MY_____ SCORE

You Have a "Date" with History!

Well, of course you'd rather have a date with that cute kid you're crazy about, but this is geography, remember, so...see how well you score with these dates! Score one point for each right answer.

(Sometimes) It Was A Very Good Year

1. 1832

2. 1900

3. 1971

4. 1634

5. 1959

6. 1996

7. 1717

8. 1836

9. 1673

10. 1848

A. Black Hawk War ended in Wisconsin

B. University of Wisconsin united 17 campuses

C. Jolliet and Marquette crossed Wisconsin and discovered the Upper Mississippi

D. Reformist Robert La Follette, Sr. was elected governor

E. St. Lawrence Seaway was opened benefiting Wisconsin ports

F. The first permanent European settlement was established

G. Wisconsin Works Program was created

H. Territory of Wisconsin was created

I. Wisconsin became the 30th state

J. Jean Nicolet explored the area

ISN'T IT YOUR NAP TIME?

YEAH! THANKS FOR REMINDING ME.

ANSWERS: 1-A; 2-D; 3-B; 4-J; 5-E; 6-G; 7-F; 8-H; 9-C; 10-I

MY SCORE ____

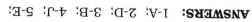

Wisconsin Festivals!

Jog on down to some of our state's fun festivals and other activities.
Score one point for each one you can match correctly. Have a great time!

Eat, Drink, & Be Merry!

1. World Championship Snowmobile Derby

2. Summerfest

3. Experimental Aircraft Association Fly-In

4. Lumberjack World Championship

5. World Championship Off-Road Races

6. Walleye Weekend

7. Hot Air Balloon Rally

8. Chocolate Festival

9. Oktoberfest

10. World Dairy Expo

A. Milwaukee

B. Crandon

C. Burlington

D. Hayward

E. Eagle River

F. La Crosse

G. Fond du Lac

H. Oshkosh

I. Hudson

J. Madison

ANSWERS: 1-E; 2-A; 3-H; 4-D; 5-B;
6-G; 7-I; 8-C; 9-F; 10-J

IT'S PARTY TIME!

MY ____ SCORE

Wisconsin
Finding Famous Residents!

You know who was you know what—but do you know who was what? Be a good resident and score a point for each person who lived in Wisconsin with what made them famous.

Fascinating and Famous Folks!

1. Georgia O'Keeffe

2. Laura Ingles Wilder

3. Frank Lloyd Wright

4. Spencer Tracy

5. Liberace

6. Jean Nicolet

7. Marguerite Henry

8. Harry Houdini

9. "Woody" Herman

10. Oshkosh

A. Born in Richland Center, he was a world-famous architect

B. Born in Pepin, she wrote popular children's stories

C. A well-known artist born in Sun Prairie

D. Wrote children's books about horses

E. Frenchman who explored Green Bay, the Fox, and Wisconsin Rivers

F. A famous actor of days gone by who was born in Milwaukee

G. Also known as "Woodrow," a big band leader and jazz musician

H. West Allis' great, world-renown pianist

I. A Menominee Indian who fought to keep tribal lands in Wisconsin

J. Famous magician who grew up in Appleton, he was notorious as an accomplished escape artist

ANSWERS: 1-C; 2-B; 3-A; 4-F; 5-H; 6-E; 7-D; 8-J; 9-G; 10-I

MY SCORE _____

Jog On Down Around Town!

Keep on jogging and see if you can score two points for each correct answer!

Jog On Down, Jog On Down the Road

1. This type of animal hibernates: _ _ _ _ Creek

2. Put this in your fireplace to make a crackling fire: _ _ _ _ ville

3. Everything turns this refreshing color in spring: _ _ _ _ _ field

4. Don't get this grit blown in your eyes! _ _ _ _ Creek

5. Like a stream or creek, often babbling: _ _ _ _ _ _ side

6. Some like Chevy and Ford, others prefer: _ _ _ _ _ _ ville

7. This comes up in the east and sets in the west: Rising _ _ _

8. The head of a kingdom: _ _ _ _ ston

9. Red delicious, Gala, Granny Smith: _ _ _ _ _ _ ton

10. Not left or right, but right in the middle: Union _ _ _ _ _ _

JUST DO IT!

MY SCORE

ANSWERS: 1-Bear Creek; 2-Woodville; 3-Greenfield; 4-Sand Creek; 5-Brookside; 6-Dodgeville; 7-Rising Sun; 8-Kingston; 9-Appleton; 10-Union Center

Wisconsin
Jog On Down Through History!

Jog (or run!) through time and find out interesting, important, and intriguing historical facts. Give yourself a point for each correct one!

1. Milwaukee was founded in 1795 as a:
   - ○ A)Trading post
   - ○ B) Fort
   - ○ C) Port

2. Wisconsin is bordered by _____ states.
   - ○ A) Five
   - ○ B) Six
   - ○ C) Four

3. Wisconsin is also referred to as:
   - ○ A) Cheese Land
   - ○ B) America's Dairyland
   - ○ C) Winter Wonderland

4. Wisconsin's first territorial governor was:
   - ○ A) Henry Dodge
   - ○ B) James Ford
   - ○ C) William Chrysler

5. Pendarvis is a group of restored stone _____ built by miners in the early 1800s located in Mineral Point.
   - ○ A) Houses
   - ○ B) Railroad Tracks
   - ○ C) Barns

6. The Yerkes Observatory at Williams Bay has the:
   - ○ A) World's smallest microscope
   - ○ B) World's largest satellite center
   - ○ C) World's largest refracting telescope

7. A wedge of land in the southern shoreline of Lake Superior is called:
   - ○ A) Door Peninsula
   - ○ B) Bayfield Peninsula
   - ○ C) Marshfield Peninsula

8. In Rhinelander, a "hodag" is a type of:
   - ○ A) Dance or get-together held in barns
   - ○ B) Hairstyle of the 1950s
   - ○ C) Mythical creature like a hairy dinosaur

9. Nekoosa and Wisconsin Rapids, once lumber-mill towns, are now known for:
   - ○ A) Danish kringles
   - ○ B) Paper-milling
   - ○ C) Cranberry production

10. Eau Claire, Menominee, Black River Falls, and La Crosse are located in:
    - ○ A) The Lower Mississippi Valley
    - ○ B) The Central Sands region
    - ○ C) The Upper Coulee region

MY SCORE _____

ANSWERS: 1-A; 2-C; 3-B; 4-A; 5-A; 6-C; 7-B; 8-C; 9-B; 10-C

Wisconsin

The Local Weatherperson–You!

Score one point for each match you make about Wisconsin's weather. (Do you get a point "weather or not" you get it right? NO!)

1. Record high temperature

2. Temperate continental

3. Maritime Tropical Gulf air mass

4. Continental Polar air mass

5. Average annual precipitation

6. Record low temperature

7. Nineteen

8. Average snowfall

9. Average July temperature

10. The Great Lakes

A. -54°F (-48°C)

B. 45 inches (114.3 cm)

C. 114°F (46°C)

D. Body of water that affects the weather greatly!

E. From the Gulf of Mexico, brings high humidity and summer heat

F. The average number of tornadoes that touch down in the state each year

G. 70°F (21°C)

H. Brings bitter-cold dry winter weather

I. 31 inches (79 cm)

J. A type of climate that can be bitterly cold with lots of snow in winter and warm and humid in the summer

ANSWERS: 1-C; 2-J; 3-E; 4-H; 5-I; 6-A; 7-F; 8-B; 9-G; 10-D

MY SCORE ____

Wisconsin
Colorful Places!

See if you can jog around Wisconsin and identify these colorful places. Score one point for each correct place you complete.

Go Over the Rainbow!

1. S _ _ _ _ _ _ Lake

2. B _ _ _ _ _ Earth

3. B _ _ _ _ _ Deer

4. W _ _ _ _ water

5. G _ _ _ _ _ Bay

6. C _ _ _ _ _ Lake

7. R _ _ granite

8. B _ _ _ _ _ River Falls

9. Hazel G _ _ _ _ _

10. G _ _ _ _ _ Lake

MY SCORE ____

Wisconsin
State Parks

Wisconsin has several great state parks to visit! Score a point for each match you make!

Have A Fun Time!

1. Devil's Lake State Park

2. Mitchell Park

3. Heritage Hill State Park

4. Aztalan State Park

5. First Capitol State Park

6. Whitefish Dunes State Park

7. Rock Island State Park

8. Perrot State Park

9. Blue Mound State Park

10. Mirror Lake State Park

A. Early Wisconsin history preserved in Green Bay

B. Largest number of mound sites

C. Oldest lighthouse in the state

D. Triple geodesic domes filled with fabulous flora (plant life)

E. Largest sand dunes in the state

F. Only state park with a swimming pool

G. Ancient pyramids built about 800 years ago

H. The state's largest state park

I. Rent a Frank Lloyd Wright cottage

J. The smallest state park, in Belmont

ANSWERS: 1-H; 2-D; 3-A; 4-G; 5-J; 6-E; 7-C; 8-B; 9-F; 10-I

Wisconsin
Let's Get Physical!

The physical characteristics, climate, and natural resources of Wisconsin's regions and communities influence their products, industries, and economic specialization. Score a point for each correct answer.

Don't Break A Sweat!

1. The Cranmoor region of Wood County has thousands of acres of:
   - ○ A) Desert
   - ○ B) Worm farms
   - ○ C) Cranberry bogs

2. Castle Rock Flowage is a:
   - ○ A) Dammed up lake in central Wisconsin
   - ○ B) Backed up bog near Door County
   - ○ C) Geological landmark on the Wisconsin River

3. Wisconsin's beautiful and varied landscape is the result of:
   - ○ A) Flowing and frozen water
   - ○ B) Extreme sunshine and warm days
   - ○ C) Desert winds and lack of rainfall

4. The lumberjack known as the mythical legend of the North Woods is:
   - ○ A) Achilles Tendon
   - ○ B) Paul Bunyan
   - ○ C) Marvin Corn

5. The St. Croix River runs along the:
   - ○ A) Western boundary with Minnesota
   - ○ B) Northeastern boundary with Michigan
   - ○ C) Southern boundary with Illinois

6. Ice covered most of Wisconsin in the Ice Ages except this part:
   - ○ A) Shift free area
   - ○ B) Driftless area
   - ○ C) Slick spot

7. In Iron County, a vein of ore stretches across the border of Wisconsin and:
   - ○ A) Iowa
   - ○ B) Michigan
   - ○ C) Illinois

8. The northernmost point in Wisconsin is:
   - ○ A) The Apostle Islands
   - ○ B) Washington Island
   - ○ C) Ashland

9. Features that describe Wisconsin's climate are:
   - ○ A) Long, cold, snowy winters
   - ○ B) Mild, warm, and sunny winters
   - ○ C) Short, lukewarm winters

10. In the mid-1800s, Wisconsin's lumber industry benefited from the construction of:
    - ○ A) Dams
    - ○ B) Railroads
    - ○ C) Major highways

MY _____ SCORE

ANSWERS: 1-C; 2-C; 3-A; 4-B; 5-A; 6-B; 7-B; 8-A; 9-A; 10-B

Wisconsin
Manimals

Score one point for each person or animal you can match with its fun fact!

Man, Oh Manimal!

1. Cranes

2. The dairy cow

3. Liberace

4. Canada geese

5. Vince Lombardi

6. "Muskie"

7. Aldo Leopold

8. Mourning dove

9. The "Badger State"

10. Harry Houdini

A. Wisconsin's state fish

B. One of the state's nicknames

C. These fly south for the winter

D. Wildlife ecologist and writer

E. A very popular milk producer

F. Flamboyant pianist born in West Allis

G. Magician and escape artist, grew up in Appleton

H. Well-known past coach of the Green Bay Packers

I. State symbol of peace

J. International Crane Foundation in Baraboo, helps with extinction difficulties

ANSWERS: 1-J; 2-E; 3-F; 4-C; 5-H; 6-A; 7-D; 8-I; 9-B; 10-G

MY SCORE ____

Wisconsin
Be A Good Sport!

Be a good sport! Score one point each by matching the person, place, or thing with the fun fact!

The Joy of Victory (or The Agony of DA FEET!)

1. Lambeau Field

2. Brewers

3. Elroy (Crazy Legs) Hirsch

4. Bucks in Milwaukee

5. Vince Lombardi

6. Bicycle race

7. Earl "Curly" Lambeau

8. Dan Jansen

9. Beth and Eric Heiden

10. Bart Starr

A. Milwaukee Professional Baseball Team

B. Began coaching the Packers in 1959

C. Chequamegon Fat Tire Festival in Cable, Wisconsin

D. A former quarterback for the Packers

E. 1984 Olympic speed skater

F. Green Bay Packers play here

G. 1968 Professional Football Hall of Famer

H. Olympic Gold Medalist speed skaters from Madison

I. Professional Basketball Team

J. Founder of the Green Bay Packers

MY SCORE _____

ANSWERS: 1-F; 2-A; 3-G; 4-I; 5-B; 6-C; 7-J; 8-E; 9-H; 10-D

HEEEY!
I'VE GOT MY OWN PAGE

Wisconsin "Jography" Towns

See how many of these town names you can complete before you tally your "Jography" score!

You Can Do It!

1. A yellow cheese: C _ _ _ _

2. An Indian weapon: T _ _ _ _ _ _ _

3. An animal that builds dams: B _ _ _ _ _

4. A man-made barrier around a yard: F _ _ _ _

5. A South American country with llamas: P _ _ _

6. Good fortune: L _ _ _

7. The national bird: E _ _ _ _

8. Simple: P _ _ _ _

9. A loud alarm: S _ _ _ _

10. A large woolly plains animal: B _ _ _ _ _ _

MY SCORE _____

ANSWERS: 1-Colby; 2-Tomahawk; 3-Beaver; 4-Fence; 5-Peru; 6-Luck; 7-Eagle; 8-Plain; 9-Siren; 10-Buffalo

LADIES AND GENTLEMEN, WE HAVE A WINNER!

OK, Jogger, How Did You Score?

SOONER OR LATER . . .
you're going to have to find out:

If you didn't score many points at all—you may not be able to find your way home and back! Try and improve your score—it will be easier the second time.

If you scored a few more points—well, maybe you really live in Timbuctu? Timbucktoo? Timbuctwo? Try Again!

If you scored a lot of points—this book was meant just for you. Don't take those shoes off! Jog, jog again 'til you can improve your score! I know you can do it!!!

Final Score _____

He won?

He won?

I won? I won!!!

Make Up Your Own Questions

Here's a place for you to write your own "Jography" questions about places and things in your own hometown.

Quiz your friends! Your parents!! Your teacher!!!

1. _____

2. _____

3. _____

4. _____

5. _____

6. _____

7. _____

8. _____

9. _____

10. _____

I THINK I'LL WRITE A BOOK!